30 DEVOTIONS
CONSISTENCY,

Faithful

publishing team

Director, Student Ministry
Ben Trueblood

Manager, Student Ministry Publishing
John Paul Basham

Editorial Team Leader
Karen Daniel

Writer
Sarah McLean

Content Editor
Stephanie Cross

Production Editor
Brooke Hill

Graphic Designer
Kaitlin Redmond

©2021 Lifeway Press®

No part of this work may be reproduced or transmitted in any form or by any means, electronic or mechanical, including photocopying and recording, or by any information storage or retrieval system, except as may be expressly permitted in writing by the publisher. Requests for permission should be addressed in writing to LifeWay Press®, One LifeWay Plaza, Nashville, TN 37234.

ISBN 978-1-0877-4431-5
Item 005831819
Dewey Decimal Classification Number: 242
Subject Heading: DEVOTIONAL LITERATURE / BIBLE STUDY AND TEACHING / GOD

Printed in the United States of America

Student Ministry Publishing
LifeWay Resources
One LifeWay Plaza
Nashville, Tennessee 37234

We believe that the Bible has God for its author; salvation for its end; and truth, without any mixture of error, for its matter and that all Scripture is totally true and trustworthy. To review LifeWay's doctrinal guideline, please visit www.lifeway.com/doctrinalguideline.

Unless otherwise noted, all Scripture quotations are taken from the Christian Standard Bible®, Copyright © 2017 by Holman Bible Publishers. Used by permission. Christian Standard Bible® and CSB® are federally registered trademarks of Holman Bible Publishers.

04
intro

05
getting started

06
God's faithfulness

30
faithful to God

44
portraits of faithfulness

72
articles and resources

table of contents

Intro

Everything God does points to who He is and how He loves us. Because He is the one true God and the very truth we seek, He cannot be anything other than what He says. His actions will always line up with His words. In a word, He is faithful.

God's faithfulness is incredibly good news for us. He is so great that His faithfulness does more and extends further than we could ever imagine. No matter what you've done or how far you've run, His faithfulness will meet you where you are. It is in His very nature to be faithful.

Because of this, every single one of His plans will be accomplished and His promises fulfilled. He sent Jesus as the ultimate assurance that He isn't just One who makes promises—He *always* keeps them. In Jesus, He has given us this greatest gift. Our right response to that is to use the life we've been given to faithfully serve Him and others.

As we walk through His Word together over the next 30 days, we'll see His faithfulness, how He has called us to be faithful, and biblical examples of what it really looks like to trust God and follow Him no matter where He leads.

God's faithfulness isn't about you. It's not about who you are, what you've done, or what you want from Him. God's faithfulness is ultimately about His character and His glory. So, to His eternal and limitless faithfulness, we devote our hearts today and forever.

getting started

This devotional contains 30 days of content, broken down into sections about faithfulness. Each day is divided into three elements—discover, delight, and display—to help you answer core questions related to Scripture.

discover

This section helps you examine the passage in light of who God is and determine what it says about your identity in relationship to Him. Included here is the daily Scripture reading, focus passage, along with illustrations and commentary to guide you as you study.

delight

In this section, you'll be challenged by questions and activities that help you see how God is alive and active in every detail of His Word and your life.

display

Here's where you take action. Display calls you to apply what you've learned through each day's study.

prayer

Each day also includes a prayer activity in one of the three main sections.

Throughout the devotional, you'll also find extra articles and activities to help you connect with the topic personally, such as such as Scripture memory verses, additional resources, and questions.

Faithful

Section 1: GOD'S FAITHFULNESS

day 1

A THOUSAND GENERATIONS

discover|

READ DEUTERONOMY 7:7-9

Know that the LORD your God is God, the faithful God who keeps his gracious covenant loyalty for a thousand generations with those who love him and keep his commands. —Deuteronomy 7:9

As we read the Bible, we discover truths about God. The pages of Scripture are all about the eternal, unchanging, and merciful God of creation. Though God is infinite, and growing in our understanding of who He is will span our entire lives, we should desire to know Him deeper through the study of His Word. By doing so, we not only know Him more, but we also grow in our affection for Him as we see how His love is demonstrated through redemptive actions. One of the most important aspects of His nature which He has revealed to us is His faithfulness.

We can define faithful as "steadfast, dedicated, dependable, and worthy of trust." By this definition, we may think of many people in our lives who are faithful. Maybe we think of our parents or teachers or coaches who have stood by us through the ups and downs of life. We can depend on them and know they are people we can lean on. Yet, God's faithfulness exceeds even the most faithful person in our lives. His faithfulness is to *a thousand generations* to those who love Him. It never wavers or grows tired. He is faithful to keep His word and stand by His promises forever. His faithfulness provides us with security and an anchor of hope when life becomes scary and uncertain.

Lifeway Girls | Devotions

delight |

Read Deuteronomy 7:7-9 again. God chose to be faithful to Israel, but not because they earned His faithfulness in any way. How does this encourage you to trust God's faithfulness in your own life?

We are called to love God and keep His commands (v. 9). How does God's faithfulness cause you to love Him more and desire to follow His commands?

display |

Take some time this week to write out ways you observe God's faithfulness. How is He showing you He is dependable, trustworthy, and steadfast? Share with your friends, parents, or pastor, and encourage them to look for God's faithfulness as well.

> **Spend some time in prayer, thanking God for His faithfulness and asking Him to allow His faithfulness to increase your love for Him. Ask Him to help you walk through this devotional with a heart that desires to love God more for His steadfast faithfulness.**

day 2

PROMISE KEEPER

discover

READ NUMBERS 23:19-23.

God is not a man, that he might lie, or a son of man, that he might change his mind. Does he speak and not act, or promise and not fulfill? —Numbers 23:19

We see God's faithfulness on full display in these verses. Despite Balak calling Balaam to curse Israel, God made it so Balaam could only bless Israel. The Lord chose Israel and promised to remain faithful to the Israelites no matter what.

God can't be anything but faithful—it's who He is. To say this another way, God's faithfulness is connected to His truthfulness. When God promises to be faithful, He doesn't break that promise because He doesn't lie. Psalm 115:1 reads, "Not to us, Lord, not to us, but to your name give glory because of your faithful love, because of your truth." God will always do what He says as He remains faithful to His Word. And those who are saved by faith in Christ can trust His Word as Jesus promised to always remain faithful to us (Matt. 28:20).

As we go throughout our days, we don't need to worry about all that life could throw at us. Israel didn't need to worry if God would abandon them to Balaam's curses. He had already promised that He would not forsake them. Just as God's faithfulness was with Israel, so will His faithfulness be with us. Israel was God's chosen people, and He made a covenant to remain faithful to them. Likewise, we are chosen in Christ, and God has promised to remain faithful to us.

Lifeway Girls | Devotions

delight

How have you seen God remain faithful to His promises in your own life? Be specific.

Why is it important that God keeps His word? How does this encourage your faith as you read the Bible?

display

Name one way you can make His faithfulness known to others and bring Him praise today.

> **Pray about ways you can declare, "What great things God has done!" in your own life. May we give glory to God for His faithfulness and remember that in Christ we are promised His faithfulness forever.**

Faithful

day 3

MERCIFUL

discover

READ LAMENTATIONS 3:22-24.

Because of the LORD's faithful love we do not perish, for his mercies never end. They are new every morning; great is your faithfulness! I say, "The LORD is my portion, therefore I will put my hope in him." —Lamentations 3:22-24

Have you ever felt like you have blown it for the last time? Maybe you see all your faults or failures and wonder if this time God has had enough. It is probably safe to assume that we have all felt like this at some point. Yet, even with all of our shortcomings, God's faithfulness assures us that His mercy will never come to an end for those who are in Christ Jesus.

The prophet Jeremiah's words in these verses were to a broken and destroyed people. The city of Jerusalem had been destroyed, and they were weeping over their sin. Still, in the midst of consequences for sin, God still declared His faithfulness and mercy. He is still the God who rescues and redeems.

His mercies are new every morning and provide us with all we need to walk in His truth. This doesn't mean we're perfect. Rather, we trust that Jesus is more than enough to not only cover our sins, but also satisfy our every desire. His faithful love provides us mercy in our times of temptation, in our times of need, and even in our times of doubt. He is our portion forever. Because of His faithful, merciful love, we hope only in Him.

delight |

What keeps you from trusting that God's faithfulness will also bring you endless mercy?

When have you experienced God's faithful mercy? Explain.

display |

As you go about your week, meditate on the mercy you receive from the Lord because of His faithfulness. Then, think about ways you can be merciful toward others. What would that look like with your family, friends, teammates, and other girls in your youth group?

> **Think about how God has been merciful to you throughout your life. Then, spend some time in prayer asking God to help you continue to trust His faithful mercy in your life.**

Faithful

day 4

LIMITLESS

discover

READ PSALM 36:5.

LORD, your faithful love reaches to heaven, your faithfulness to the clouds.

When we look up toward the night sky, we see the great expanse of the stars, moon, and even planets. Sometimes the moon is so large it looks like it could collide with Earth. But did you know the moon is over 230,000 miles from our planet?[1] You could fit 30 Earths within that distance! Yet, God's faithfulness reaches even beyond the outer edges of the universe. There is no distance or space that God's faithfulness will not extend to and beyond.

Looking up to heaven reminded the psalmist of God's faithfulness. As the heavens go on and on, so does God's faithfulness. Even more, God's faithfulness has no limit because He is an infinite God who is not confined by space or time. He is so far above us, we cannot fully comprehend the greatness of His faithfulness to us.

But the God of the heavens reaches out to us and offers us His faithful love. He chose to give His only Son to show His love for us and allow us to experience His limitless faithfulness. The promises of God's faithfulness in Christ extend to eternity and will never fail us. Let us rejoice and give Him thanks for being a good Father whose faithfulness has no limit.

delight

Why does the faithfulness of God have no limit? (Hint: See Isa. 40:28)

How does Jesus' death and resurrection assure us that God's faithfulness will last forever?

display

How can you choose to mirror God's unending faithfulness to others? Think about a girl in your life who may feel alone. Write down one way you can be there for her this week. Encourage her with the Scripture you've read in today's devotion.

> **Give thanks to God through prayer as you think about how God's faithfulness has no limit. Reflect on how He's been faithful to you in limitless ways.**

day 5

GOD'S PLANS ARE FAITHFUL

discover

READ ISAIAH 25.

*L*ORD*, you are my God; I will exalt you. I will praise your name, for you have accomplished wonders, plans formed long ago, with perfect faithfulness.*
—Isaiah 25:1

Every day we make many plans. Sometimes we make routine plans, like deciding what we will have for breakfast or what we will wear to school. Other days we make distant plans, like where we might go to college or how we will celebrate our birthday. Sometimes our plans turn out how we would like, and other times they fail. Our failed plans remind us that we are not in ultimate control.

But the Lord's plans are always executed with perfect faithfulness and are fulfilled exactly as He has established. Not only are God's plans faithful, but He also determined them long ago. We can trust His every plan will come to fruition because every word of the Lord stands firm and true, never returning void (Isa. 55:11).

Isaiah's words remind us that God's long established plans will always be accomplished because of His perfect faithfulness. The God of our salvation set in motion the plan of redemption through Jesus Christ, by which His faithfulness has been fulfilled. Though the future glory of a new creation has not yet come, we still trust that God's plan will be fulfilled. And like Isaiah said, the perfect faithfulness of God should cause our hearts to exalt and praise Him. His plans are always for our good and His glory.

delight |

Read Isaiah 25:9. Should we lose trust in God's faithfulness toward His plans even if it requires waiting? Explain.

Even though you don't know the exact plans God has for your life, how does His faithfulness help you trust Him?

display |

God has many plans for our lives, and He will be faithful to them all. But He has called us to share in the plan of salvation by sharing Jesus with others. Name a girl in your life who needs to hear the good news of the gospel.

How is God faithful to be with you as you share the good news?

> **Take a moment and remember how God's plan has unfolded in your life. Even if there have been difficulties, remember how He's been there with you as you've walked through them. Pray that God would give you the opportunity to share with others how His plans have affected you.**

Faithful

day 6

EVEN IF...

discover

READ 2 TIMOTHY 2:8-13.

... if we are faithless, he remains faithful, for he cannot deny himself.
—2 Timothy 2:13

There have been some "giants" of faith throughout history. We look to people like Paul the apostle, Martin Luther the reformer, Charles Spurgeon the prince of preachers, Amy Carmichael the missionary, Corrie Ten Boom the heroine, and many more. These men and women lived extraordinary lives of faith that have inspired others to trust the Lord. But even the most faith-filled followers of Jesus have at times been faithless. No human, except for our Savior Jesus Christ, has walked this earth in perfect faithfulness. We are fallen, finite, limited in understanding, and unable to be what only God can be.

At times, we might be discouraged by our lack of faithfulness. We might find ourselves in circumstances where we are either tempted to sin or where we fail to be obedient to God. We might be going through a time of suffering, as is the context of these verses, and find our faith to be weak as doubt rises in our hearts. Nevertheless, God is not changed by our responses or our lack of faithfulness. He will always remain faithful toward those who are His through Jesus. Still, we can't ignore the warning in verse 12. Remember that when we come to faith in Jesus, we are no longer our own. We were bought with the precious blood of Christ, and we become one with Him by faith.

delight |

When have you found yourself to be faithless? Do you become discouraged by your faithlessness? Explain.

How does God's faithfulness help us endure everything (v. 10)?

display |

Spend some time meditating on 2 Timothy 2:13 and commit it to memory. When you find yourself falling into sin or reacting in a faithless manner, allow this verse to remind you of God's faithfulness toward you and encourage you to keep trusting in Him.

> **Thank God for being faithful toward us in every circumstance. We can find mercy and forgiveness even when we are faithless because God's faithfulness will be there to secure our future. God's faithfulness is a sure and steady gift of endless love.**

day 7

CONFESSION

discover

READ 1 JOHN 1:8-10.

If we confess our sins, he is faithful and righteous to forgive us our sins and to cleanse us from all unrighteousness. —1 John 1:9

One thing we have in common with all of humanity is the reality of our sinfulness. All have fallen short of the glory of God (Rom. 3:23). So, our sin must be removed for us to be made right before God.

In His grace, God provided a way for sin to be atoned for and forgiveness to be made available. Sin was paid for by the precious blood of Jesus Christ—our sin is only removed when we trust in Jesus' death and resurrection by faith. We exercise this faith through the confession of our sin and acknowledgment that Jesus alone can cleanse us of all unrighteousness.

When we have believed in our hearts our need for Jesus and confessed our sin, then God will be faithful to forgive us. Not only does this mean He will forgive our past sins, but He will also forgive our present and future sins.

But if Jesus has paid for our sins and we believe in Him, why do we need to keep confessing our sins? Our confession of sin is an honest admission of our continual need for Christ and how we also continue to fight against sin. Because of Jesus, we can freely come before the Lord, without fear or condemnation, knowing He will forgive us.

Lifeway Girls | Devotions

delight |

Have you ever been reluctant to forgive someone when they have wronged you? What does this say about our faithfulness versus the faithfulness of God?

How is God's faithfulness to forgive sins for all time (past, present, and future) shown through Jesus? (Hint: see Heb. 9:26-28)

display |

God will always be faithful to forgive our sins. Think about sins you need to confess to Him.

You can also confess your sins to another believer, asking her to help hold you accountable. An accountability partner is another godly girl who walks alongside you as you live out your faith, studies Scripture with you, encourages you to live in God-honoring ways, and confronts you when you don't. Prayerfully consider who might be a good accountability partner.

Also, be mindful of how you can forgive others, emulating the faithfulness of God to forgive.

> **Examine your heart and see if there is any unconfessed sin in your life. Then, pray and ask for forgiveness. If we simply live without ever confessing sin, we may begin to think we have no sin. Confession is how we remember the gospel and profess our continued faith in our Savior.**

day 8

THE WAY OUT

discover

READ 1 CORINTHIANS 10:1-13.

No temptation has come upon you except what is common to humanity. But God is faithful; he will not allow you to be tempted beyond what you are able, but with the temptation he will also provide the way out so that you may be able to bear it. —1 Corinthians 10:13

In these verses, Paul explained that we avoid giving in to temptation through God's faithfulness. He will not allow us to be tempted beyond what we are able to bear, and He will provide a way out. It is His steadfast faithfulness that helps us when we find ourselves in situations in which we are tempted to sin.

God's faithfulness comes to us in our time of need through Jesus. When we are tempted to sin, we find the help we need by knowing Jesus is with us and that He sympathizes with our weakness (Heb. 4:15). We can come to the Lord in confidence because of what Christ has done on our behalf and find grace and strength to fight temptation.

God has also been faithful to give us His Word so we may be equipped to battle any temptation. Just as Jesus used Scripture against Satan in the wilderness (Matt. 4:1-11; Luke 4:1-13), so can we hold fast to and believe God's Word over the lies of the world. God's faithfulness has given us everything we need to run from sin and run to His grace.

delight |

What Scripture has God given you to fight against sin?

How have you seen God's faithfulness at work when you have been tempted?

display |

God promises that He will always provide a way out of temptation, and His Word is a powerful weapon against sin. Choose a Bible verse to memorize that will help you when you're tempted. Maybe you are quick to gossip, or maybe you struggle with anger. Whatever it may be, God's Word is an extension of His faithfulness and a means to fight again sin. Write out the area you struggle with and the verse you chose to help you when you're tempted in that area.

> **Take some time to pray and examine some areas where you are tempted to sin. How can you begin to turn to God's faithfulness to provide a way out? Ask Him to show you the way out.**

Faithful

day 9

GUARD YOU FROM EVIL

discover

READ 2 THESSALONIANS 3:1-5.

But the Lord is faithful; he will strengthen and guard you from the evil one.
—2 Thessalonians 3:3

God is sovereign and ultimately in control of our world, but Satan and his evil forces are at work in this world to sway people from following Jesus. Not all people have faith and are therefore under the rule of the evil one (2 Thess. 3:2). Such people take part in wicked and evil deeds, which may harm those who are in Christ. They are opposed to the gospel and working according to the ruler of disobedience (Eph. 2:2).

But as Christ followers, we don't have to fear the evil one or wicked people. While some may seek to harm us, ridicule our faith, and discredit us, we have a God who is faithful to guard us against the evil one. Now, Paul wasn't saying you won't have troubles. Jesus made it clear that His followers would have trouble and would be hated by those who love this world (Matt. 10:22; John 16:33). Despite what evil deeds may happen here on earth, God will stand guard against the evil one and give us strength during tough times.

Paul encouraged us to look to God's love and Christ's endurance when we find ourselves affected by evil schemes (v. 5). Christ endured evil for our sins, and His Father was faithful to raise Him to life again. We have that same promise of God's faithfulness and can confidently endure trials by trusting He will always be faithful.

Lifeway Girls | Devotions

delight

How does Jesus' death and resurrection give you confidence in God's faithful promise to guard us against the evil one?

How would you encourage another believer to trust God's faithfulness when she suffers?

display

Paul asked the Thessalonians to pray for their deliverance from evil people. Name a girl you can you pray for who might be enduring a trial caused by the wickedness of others.

> Ask God to guard and strengthen your brothers and sisters in Christ. Ask Him to comfort them as they walk through these dark days, to help them rest assured that He is in control and that His love for them never changes.

Faithful

day 10

CALLED BY FAITHFULNESS

discover

READ 1 CORINTHIANS 1:4-9.

God is faithful; you were called by him into fellowship with his Son, Jesus Christ our Lord. —1 Corinthians 1:9

The ways of the world attempt to lead us in many different directions. Sometimes we might be tempted to act a certain way because we are influenced by our friends. Other times we might feel like we should believe the ideas of our society just because they are popular. But the world's ideas are constantly changing because the ways of the world are not grounded in truth. God alone holds all truth, and in His faithfulness, He's always leading us to what is true—namely the Truth, Jesus Christ.

God has been faithful since the garden of Eden to lead people into fellowship with Himself through grace and by faith in the promise of the Messiah. And He continued to be faithful to that promise until eventually the Messiah did come. The call of salvation has been gifted to everyone through Jesus, and the Lord continues to lead sinners to Himself by way of the cross.

God wants all people to repent and come to faith in Christ (2 Pet. 2:3). He has made salvation possible for all people, if only they confess their sin and believe in the Lord Jesus Christ. Paul exhorted the Corinthian church to remember God's faithfulness to them. He provided an example of God's faithfulness by reminding them of how He called them to salvation in Christ and how He will continue to sustain their faith until Jesus returns. We, too, can cling to that promise and trust God's faithful leading.

Lifeway Girls | Devotions

delight |

How did God's faithfulness help you recognize your sin and grasp your need for repentance?

Why did Paul assure the Corinthians of their eternal salvation (v. 8)? How does this relate to God's faithfulness?

display |

God is faithful to lead sinners to Jesus. How might God use you to take part in His faithfulness by sharing the gospel with a girl who does not know Jesus? How can you encourage the girls in your life who know Jesus to rest in His faithfulness?

> **Spend some time in prayer over these questions, then ask God to show you a way to put them into action this week.**

Faithful

day 11

HOLD ON

discover

READ HEBREWS 10:19-25.

Let us hold on to the confession of our hope without wavering, since he who promised is faithful. —Hebrews 10:23

We can most likely all attest to broken promises in our lives. People say one thing, but do another. Sometimes, the broken promises are not intentional or spiteful. Still, we know the disappointment a broken promise can cause.

Quite the opposite is true about our God. He is not only a promise maker, but a promise keeper. When God declares He will do something, He will do it. This is why the author of Hebrews said we can "hold on to the confession of our hope without wavering." Our God has promised, and He will be faithful to uphold what He has promised. Knowing that we have a God who will do what He says should cause us to live in light of that hope. If God tells us that in Christ we can never be separated from Him, we have forgiveness, and we have a High Priest who makes intercession for us, then we should be confident to give our lives in service of Him.

Our hope in His faithful promises stirs our hearts toward good works and encouraging others to do the same. We joyfully live for the Lord because we love who He is and what He has done for us. His faithfulness assures us that despite what we face in this life, everything we do for His glory will reap eternal blessings, and we will always have the hope of our salvation.

delight

Why should God's faithfulness stir you toward good works?

How can you encourage others toward good works as well? What might you say to them to assure them of God's faithfulness?

display

Put your answer to the second question from this week into practice. Write out one way you can encourage other girls to good works as a result of God's faithfulness.

> **Give thanks to God for His faithfulness, and ask Him to give you a heart that desires to be faithful to Him with your life. Let us also ask God to give us hearts that desire to be faithful to Him just as He has been faithful to us.**

Faithful

If we are faithless, he remains faithful, for he cannot deny himself.

2 TIMOTHY 2:13

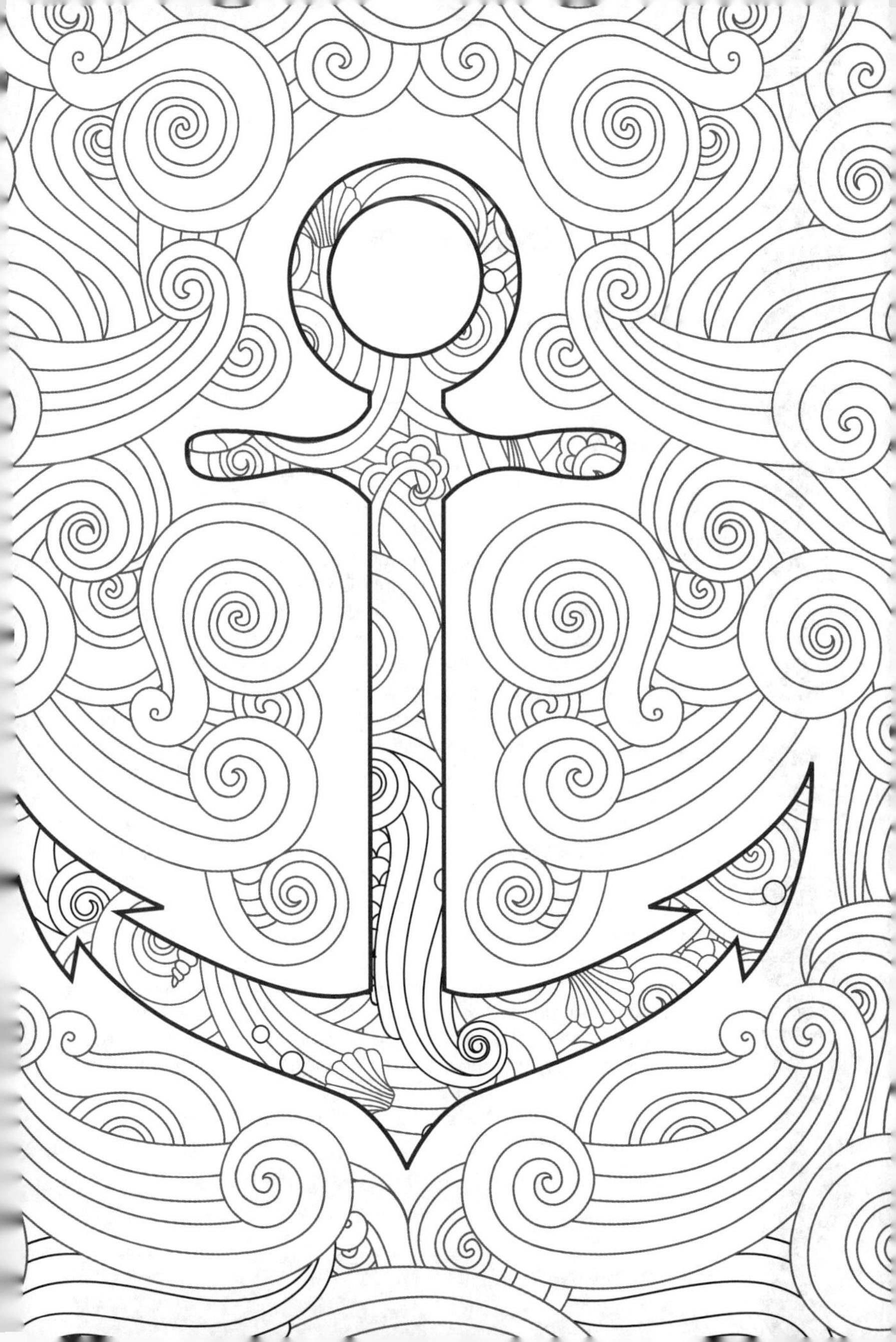

day 12

FAITHFUL IN WORSHIP

discover

READ 1 SAMUEL 12:20-24.

Above all, fear the Lord and worship Him faithfully with all your heart; consider the great things he has done for you. —1 Samuel 12:24

What are some things you're faithful to? Are you dedicated to a certain team? Or are you a faithful friend through good and tough times? Each of us can find ways we show faithfulness. There are many ways we give our time, talents, and affection toward people or things that demonstrate faithfulness. But we must be careful to not let these good gifts become the ultimate object of our faithfulness. Rather, our ultimate object of faithfulness should be our worship of our heavenly Father.

Today's verses direct our hearts to use our faithfulness to worship God. Above all, our Creator is to have complete devotion and all of our affections. Worship is how we show our faithfulness to God by making everything about His glory because we love Him more than anything else. Thus, we love God with all our hearts, minds, souls, and strength, and follow His ways above our own.

The concept of worship is not just going to church, reading the Bible, and singing praise songs. As Paul said, "whatever you do, do everything for the glory of God" (1 Cor. 10:31). We can choose to be faithful to God and worship Him in all of life's moments. Our faithfulness is only a small reflection of God's faithfulness to us. It is only because of God's faithful love that we can demonstrate faithfulness to Him.

delight

What things might try to steal your faithful worship away from God? How can you guard your heart to delight in God above all else? (Hint: See Phil. 3:8 and Col. 3:5)

How does God's faithfulness to you increase your desire to worship Him?

display

Think back on answered prayers and times when God has been faithful to you. List three instances of how God has honored your requests and how He has been faithful to make you a faithful worshiper of Him.

> Pray that God would center your heart on faithful worship to Him. Then ask Him to put to death anything that seeks to take His rightful place of worship in our hearts.

Faithful

day 13

LITTLE AND GREAT THINGS

discover

READ MATTHEW 25:14-30.

His master said to him, "Well done, good and faithful servant! You were faithful over a few things; I will put you in charge of many things. Share your master's joy." —Matthew 25:21

Think about all that God has given you—both your things and your abilities. Did God give you a talent for artistry? Do you have resources at your disposal such as a home, a car, or food? Are you skilled in certain subjects or sports? Like the parable you just read, we have all been given certain "talents" from God. Our talents may differ, but they all are valuable and should be invested wisely.

It is important to note that Jesus said talents are *given* to us. We did not earn them. Since they are gifts, we are called to use them in honor of the Giver. He has been faithful to provide what we need, and we must be faithful to steward our gifts to help build His kingdom. Just as the first two servants were entrusted with specific talents and sought to invest them wisely, so should we seek to invest our resources in ways God will use for His glory.

Jesus also reminded us that we don't all have the same number of talents. Some may have more, some may have less. Whether we are faithful over little or a lot, we can be assured that our faithfulness will produce joy. God will be pleased with our service, and we find joy in His pleasure. Knowing our faithfulness is being used to make much of our Savior should cause us to rejoice.

Lifeway Girls | Devotions

delight |

What are talents and resources God has given you?

In what ways does faithfulness to God's gifts bring you joy?

display |

Using the list you made from the first question, create a plan to invest those talents in ways God can multiply them. Maybe you have neighbors who are in need of your specific talents. Maybe your church has a missions opportunity where your talents could be used. God has given you valuable talents, and He wants you to invest them wisely.

> **Ask God to help you to be a faithful steward of the gifts He has given you. Regardless of if you have a lot of talents or a few, ask Him to help you use whatever it is you have for His kingdom and glory.**

day 14

HUMBLE FAITHFULNESS

discover

READ PSALM 31:23-24.

Love the Lord, all his faithful ones. The Lord protects the loyal, but fully repays the arrogant. Be strong, and let your heart be courageous, all you who put your hope in the Lord.

David began Psalm 31 with a cry for help. He needed God to rescue him, and he called for God's protection from his adversaries. He was afflicted, troubled, and distressed because there were people who conspired against him. He was mocked, ridiculed, and was the center of gossip from others. Life wasn't going very well for David during that time. Perhaps you can relate. Maybe you have felt alone and in a place of desperation.

This psalm was most likely written when David was being persecuted and pursued by Saul. He was on the run and in fear for his life. Yet, David did not rely on his own strength, cunningness, or past accomplishments. Remember, this was the same David who slayed lions, killed the mighty Goliath, and rode gallantly into many battles. He was a warrior. Yet, David recognized it was the Lord's strength, not his own, that brought him courage. He was faithful to depend on the Lord and turned away from an arrogant heart.

Likewise, we must love the Lord through faithfulness to Him and resist the temptation to boast in our own strength, wisdom, or accolades. Faithfulness requires humility because it showcases God as the One we depend on for everything. The arrogant deny their need of God and will not be able to stand against Him in the end.

delight

Where might you struggle with arrogance? How does God's faithfulness to you help you fight this temptation?

How does Jesus' example of faithfulness encourage you to be faithful? (See Phil. 2:8)

display

Humility and faithfulness go hand in hand. Just as Jesus served us with His humble faithfulness, we are called to use our faithfulness to think of others before ourselves. How can you humbly serve the girls in your life this week?

> **Arrogance only thinks of self and ways to boast. But in humble faithfulness, we hope and trust in the Lord Almighty. Pray about ways God can use your humble faithfulness to exalt Him and serve others.**

day 15

FAITHFULNESS TO HIS CHURCH

discover

READ HEBREWS 10:24-25.

And let us consider one another in order to provoke love and good works, not neglecting to gather together, as some are in the habit of doing, but encouraging each other, and all the more as you see the day approaching.

If you have ever been to a wedding, you know the anticipation on the groom's face as he awaits his bride. He is eager, excited, and longing for his beautiful bride to walk down the aisle. And when he sees her, every part of him lights up with joy. But before the bride can walk down the aisle, she must make herself ready. No bride wants to marry her husband with messed up hair or a tattered dress. She wants to look beautiful for her soon-to-be husband.

In a similar way, the church is the bride of Christ. One day, we will present ourselves to Him in perfect unity. In anticipation of that day, we want to make ourselves ready. We want to adorn ourselves with the godly characteristics which emulate our Groom and see His joy in us when we meet Him face to face. And it is through our faithfulness to His church that we best prepare ourselves.

If we have been justified by the blood of Christ, then we become a part of His body—the church. As such, we are called to faithfulness to His church. In our faithfulness, we do not neglect to meet together. We make the act of corporate worship a priority in our lives. We come together to build up one another and to encourage each other toward good works. Through our faithful attendance, service, and giving, we are helping to make ourselves ready for Christ's return.

Lifeway Girls | Devotions

delight

Name a few girls in your local church body who you can spur toward good works and encourage.

How are you showing your faithfulness to God's church? In what ways can you improve on your faithfulness?

display

Choose one or two girls in your church that you can love and encourage this week. List two tangible ways you can show your faithfulness to these girls.

> **Spend some time in prayer thanking God for your church body and asking Him to help you to be faithful to it. If you do not have a local church where you attend regularly, spend some time in prayer asking God to show you the place where you need to unite your life with other believers. It's not about checking "present" on an attendance box. It's about living life with other believers, learning, growing, and being faithful to Him and to one another, together.**

Faithful

day 16

TO THE END

discover

READ MATTHEW 10:16-25, 28.

You will be hated by everyone because of my name. But the one who endures to the end will be saved. —Matthew 10:22

This is a sobering passage for Christ followers. While Jesus was speaking directly to His disciples, He is speaking to us as well. We might not be flogged in a synagogue or held on trial, but we will face troubles as followers of Jesus. Many Christians around the world and even in the United States are persecuted for their faithfulness to Christ. Despite the persecution, we have the promise of salvation if we endure to the end.

It's a struggle to remain faithful when you are under intense persecution or suffering. We may be tempted to turn away or reject Christ when difficulties come. But those who are faithful will have endurance through such opposition. And where does our endurance come from?

When we are in times of suffering or trials, we look to Jesus and remember all that He endured on our behalf. Then, we are strengthened to endure by knowing He has secured our salvation. We know His suffering was far greater than anything we could possibly go through. But we also find that Jesus' words in verse 28 explain why those who are faithful endure to the end: it's because they fear the Lord more than they fear man. When our love for God is greater than our fear of anything man can do, we prove our faithfulness and will be able to endure to the end.

Lifeway Girls | Devotions

delight |

When have you ever experienced or heard of someone else experiencing persecution because of their faith in Christ?

How does your faith in Jesus help you endure hardships?

display |

The point of this passage is to help you understand that we may face persecution for our faith, but God will be with us as we walk through it. Anyone who quits a race before they cross the finish line does not get credit for having run it. Since you have begun your race as a follower of Christ, keep running to the end, knowing He's with you as you go. Find a sticky note or index card and write on it *He's with me to the end*. Then place that note in a prominent place to be reminded that He loves you and is with you.

> **Spend some time praying for the persecuted church scattered all around the world. Ask God to comfort those who are facing difficulties and trials on account of their faith in Him. Then pray that they would live out this verse: "Forgetting what is behind and reaching forward to what is ahead, I pursue as my goal the prize promised by God's heavenly call in Christ Jesus" (Phil. 3:13b-14).**

Faithful

day 17

FAITHFUL TO SHARE THE GOSPEL

discover

READ MATTHEW 28:16-20.

"Go, therefore, and make disciples of all nations, baptizing them in the name of the Father and of the Son and of the Holy Spirit, teaching them to observe everything I have commanded you. And remember, I am with you always, to the end of the age." —Matthew 28:19-20

Charles Spurgeon once said in a sermon he gave, "Have you no wish for others to be saved? Then you are not saved yourself. Be sure of that."[2] While Spurgeon is known for being terse in his speech, this is a question all Christians should ask themselves. If our hearts do not desire to see the lost come to faith in Christ, then maybe our hearts are not under the grace of the gospel. Once the Holy Spirit comes upon us, we should long for unbelievers to know and believe in the only Savior, Jesus Christ.

Not only should it be a desire, but sharing the gospel is a command given to us by Jesus. In the verses you read, Jesus' time on earth was about to come to an end. But during His time here, He fulfilled His mission. Not only did Jesus die and rise again, but He made disciples, taught about repentance and faith, and was baptized. Everything Jesus calls us to, He also did. He was faithful to fulfill the Great Commission, and now we follow in His footsteps and seek to be faithful as well.

Our faithfulness to the Great Commission comes first and foremost through our faithfulness to Jesus. In our love for Him, we obey and decide to be faithful to all He has commanded us.

Lifeway Girls | Devotions

delight |

Name the girls in your life who need to hear the good news of the gospel. How can you share the gospel with them in both word and action?

What is difficult for you about sharing the gospel? Do you ever feel ill-equipped? Explain. (Read Rom. 1:16 and 2 Tim. 1:7-8)

display |

If you are nervous to share the gospel with others, take heart! You are in good company. Memorize 2 Timothy 1:7-8 and allow it to be an encouragement to you as you strive to share the gospel with others. It's not easy, but remember that God calls us to be faithful to the task, not responsible for the result.

> **Spend some time in prayer asking God to open the hearts of those who need to hear the gospel and to provide you with opportunities to share.**

Faithful

⁷ For God has not given us a spirit of fear, but one of power, love, and sound judgment.

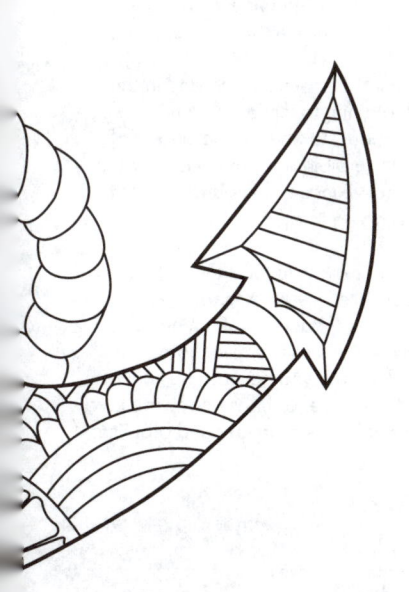

⁸ So don't be ashamed of the testimony about our Lord, or of me his prisoner. Instead, share in suffering for the gospel, relying on the power of God.

2 TIMOTHY 1:7-8

day 18

FAITH + OBEDIENCE

discover

READ GENESIS 12:1-4.

So Abram went, as the Lord had told him, and Lot went with him. Abram was seventy-five years old when he left Haran. —Genesis 12:4

During the remaining weeks of this devotional, we will be examining the lives of people who showed faithfulness. While Christ is our supreme and perfect example of a life of faithfulness, we can also learn from others who walked before us and see how the Lord worked in their lives to produce faithfulness. Let's start with Abraham and explore the ways he was faithful to God.

Abraham's (or Abram in these verses) first action recorded in the Bible is one of obedience. God told him to leave his home and go to Canaan. We're not told much about Abraham's knowledge of the Lord prior to this chapter, but the Bible does make it clear that he trusted the word of God. His obedience was grounded in faith in who God is and what God was going to do.

We, too, are called to show our faithfulness to God through our obedience. We obey God because, like Abraham, we know He is a God who can be trusted. Even though Abraham had to leave behind family, give up the comforts of a familiar home, and become an alien in a foreign land, he obeyed because he knew God's promises could be trusted. Likewise, when we obey the Lord and follow His Word, we are trusting in His character and promises.

delight |

What is most striking to you about Abraham's obedience? Why might it have been difficult for you to obey a call like that? Explain.

Why are both faith and obedience necessary to display faithfulness to God?

display |

God blessed the world through Abraham's faith-filled obedience. God can use our obedience as well to bring others to Christ, sanctify us, and make His glory known. We show God is most supreme and our greatest treasure when we obey him by faith. As we live in faithful obedience, we model the life of Christ and become more like Him. Can you think of one area you might struggle with obedience to God? What is one way this week you can be faithful to obey in this area of struggle in your life?

> **Spend some time in prayer, asking God to help you have the faith to obey Him. Then seek to put your faith into practice through faithful obedience to Him.**

Faithful

day 19

WHEREVER YOU GO

discover

READ GENESIS 13:14-18.

So Abram moved his tent and went to live near the oaks of Mamre at Hebron, where he built an altar to the LORD. —Genesis 13:18

We have the accessibility to travel in various ways to various places all over the world. We can take the bus to school; we may fly to another continent on a vacation; or we can walk to the park. Sometimes we have to move and start over in another city because our parents took a new job. Despite where we go or need to travel, we are called to be faithful to God wherever we find ourselves.

Abraham was no stranger to the nomadic life. From the time God called him from his home in Ur, he visited 17 different locations on his way to the land of Canaan.[3] Not only was Abraham faithful to obey God's command to travel, but he chose to be faithful to God despite where he lived. We must remember that the lands Abraham traveled through were inhabited by pagan people. Abraham was not without sin, but he was faithful to worship the Lord God alone and turn away from the culture's idols. No matter if he was in Hebron or in Sodom, Abraham showed his faithfulness to God alone.

We can remain faithful to God no matter where we find ourselves. We can choose to share the gospel and remain faithful to God's commands whether we are in Asia or New York. God is omnipresent and will continue to be faithful to us in every place we go. Our faithfulness to Him is not contingent on our location, but on our love to Him through the power of the Holy Spirit in us.

Lifeway Girls | Devotions

delight

Are there any locations (school, sports, new cities, stores, etc.) that have tested your faithfulness to God? Explain.

Is there any place God is calling you to go? How can you be faithful to both obey this call and show faithfulness to God wherever He calls you?

display

Think of all the places you go each week (the store, sports practice, school, home, friend's house, church, etc). How can you show your faithfulness to God in these places? List the top three places you go and write an idea of how you can practice faithfulness to Him this week beside each.

Think of two godly girls you know who go to different places than you. List one way you can encourage each of them to practice faithfulness in those places.

> **Spend some time in prayer asking God to draw you to whole-hearted devotion to Him no matter where you find yourself.**

Faithful

day 20

EVEN WHEN IT'S TOUGH

discover

READ GENESIS 15:1-6.

Abram believed the Lord, and he credited it to him as righteousness.
—Genesis 15:6

If we are honest, we would all agree that we would like to avoid difficulties in life. We would prefer for life to go our way and for it to be relatively easy. But anyone who has lived on this earth for more than a few years knows this is not how it works. We do have some easy, carefree moments, but we are also met with difficult ones. When those tough moments arise, how do we respond?

Abraham models the response of believing God even when faced with the impossible. When God first called Abraham from Ur, He promised to bless all nations through him. Yet, Abraham still had no offspring. In fact, his only heir was a slave in his household. Still, God reminded Abraham of His promise by showing him that his offspring would be as numerous as the stars in the sky. Abraham's response is how we should all respond when faced with difficulties—he chose to believe God. Despite the fact that he and his wife were old and the idea of having a child seemed crazy, God saw Abraham's faith and declared him righteous.

We will encounter tough times in this life. We will enter into circumstances that are beyond our control and seem impossible. But we can choose to remain faithful by trusting God even when life is difficult. Our ultimate trust is found in the death and resurrection of Jesus, by which we find the faithfulness to keep believing God no matter our circumstances.

Lifeway Girls | Devotions

delight

When have tough times tested your faithfulness to God?

How do God's promises encourage your faithfulness to believe even when life is difficult?

display

Read Romans 8:35-39. If you have trusted in Jesus, then you have a secure future where nothing can separate you from Him. This is a promise we can trust in and one that helps us to remain faithful when we face hard times. Write these verses on a card or in a note and share them with someone this week.

Write out the words *I choose to believe God*. You can create an artistic poster, design a print on a computer, or write out the words using your favorite color on a blank index card. Place the words where you'll see them often as a reminder to believe God no matter what's going on in your life.

> **If you're walking through a tough time right now, pray for God to help you trust in Him. If you know of someone who is in the midst of a challenging season, pray that their faith would be rooted in God.**

day 21

EVERYTHING

discover

READ GENESIS 22:1-18.

"Because you have done this thing and have not withheld your only son, I will indeed bless you and make your offspring as numerous as the stars of the sky and the sand on the seashore. Your offspring will possess the city gates of their enemies." —Genesis 22: 16b-17

What is most precious to you? For some of us it might be a tangible object such as a gaming system, money, or clothes. For others, our most prized possession may be something intangible, like beauty, popularity, or intelligence. Usually, we can determine what is precious to us if we imagine it being taken away. If something being removed from our life causes fear or worry, then it is usually something we value greatly.

God tested Abraham's faithfulness by asking Him to bring his son, Isaac, as an offering to Him. Isaac was Abraham's most precious gift—the son whom he had waited and waited for. And God asked Abraham to give him up. But Abraham had walked with God and knew God could be trusted. He had seen the promise of an heir come true, and he believed in the covenantal promise God made with him. Abraham was willing to give everything to God because even though he loved his son, he loved God more.

Abraham proved his faithfulness by believing God would provide. And God did provide a substitute to replace Isaac—a ram. Abraham had proven he revered God more than anything else in the world—even his precious son.

Lifeway Girls | Devotions

delight

Is it possible to remain faithful to God by clinging tightly to earthly treasures? Why or why not? Explain.

Jesus said, "For where your treasure is, there your heart will be also" (Matt. 6:21). What "treasure" in your heart might God ask you to surrender to Him?

How could this treasure become an idol and threaten your faithfulness to God alone?

display

In this story, we see the foreshadowing of God's sacrifice on our behalf. He gave His one and only Son—His most precious gift—so we could have eternal life. Jesus willingly laid down His life, and He calls us to do the same. When we surrender all to Him through faith, we are declaring Him to be most precious. Complete the following thought: _____ is incredibly precious to me. (You can fill in the blank with a person's name, an item, or even things like influence and status.) Now, write out: *I will declare God as my greatest treasure even above _____.*

> **Ask God to search your heart for anything else you may need to surrender to Him. Then, pray that God would help you have the courage to willingly give it over to Him, even if it is most precious to you, so He can be your greatest treasure.**

Faithful

day 22

GOD AND FAMILY

discover

READ RUTH 1:8-18.

But Ruth replied: Don't plead with me to abandon you or to return and not follow you. For wherever you go, I will go, and wherever you live, I will live; your people will be my people, and your God will be my God. —Ruth 1:16

As we continue to unpack our study of faithfulness, Ruth helps us uncover the importance of being faithful to both God and family. After her husband's death, Ruth had to decide either to go with her mother-in-law, Naomi, to a foreign land, or stay with her people in Moab. She chose to remain faithful to Naomi and to make the God of Israel her God as well.

Ruth decided it was worth it to faithfully follow Naomi and the Lord. She vowed to remain faithful to them for the rest of her days (v. 18). If she remained in Moab, she may have been able to remarry easily and not have to worry about the unknowns of a new home, but she believed faithfulness mattered. Her love for Naomi and God was made evident by her faithfulness and her willingness to leave behind the comforts of home.

While we may not be placed in the same situation as Ruth, we do have the opportunity to show faithfulness to God and our families. We can choose to keep our word when our families are expecting us to do something. We can choose to love one another even when tensions arise and family life may be challenging. We can seek to be obedient to our parent's wishes even if we do not agree with their decisions. And we can choose to be faithful to God through our faithfulness to our families.

Lifeway Girls | Devotions

delight

How has God shown faithfulness to your family? How have you shown faithfulness to your family?

Colossians 3:18-25 explains how a Christian household should function. How is faithfulness to God shown through sacrificial love to family?

display

How can you show your faithfulness to your family? Think of one practical way you can display faithfulness to each of your family members this week. Write their name below and your idea next to it.

Think about your extended family. How can you specifically show faithfulness to the women in your family this week? Choose two of your closest female relatives and write out one practical way you can be faithful to them this week.

> **Ask God to prepare your heart to display faithfulness to Him and your family this week. Then ask Him to help you carry out your practical ideas of how you can be faithful to your family.**

day 23

BLESSED TO BE A BLESSING

discover

READ RUTH 2:1-12.

"May the LORD reward you for what you have done, and may you receive a full reward from the LORD God of Israel, under whose wings you have come for refuge." —Ruth 2:11-12

One of the customs established in Hebrew law was God's command to allow the poor and foreigners to glean leftover grain from the fields (Lev. 19:9-10; 23:22; Deut. 24:19-20). Ruth and Naomi were both widows and relied upon this custom to provide food. We see Ruth showing faithfulness again to her mother-in-law by humbly working in the fields to bring home grain. Though this was a humiliating practice, her faithfulness to her mother-in-law was recognized by the owner of the field, Boaz.

Boaz commended Ruth's faithfulness not only for gleaning from the fields, but also for how she left her native land to care for Naomi. He saw her hard work and offered her protection while she continued to glean from his field. Then, he called upon the Lord to reward her for her faithfulness. He recognized that she had not only been faithful to Naomi, but also to God.

Just as Boaz recognized Ruth's faithfulness, so does the Lord. His providential hand is woven throughout this story, and because Ruth remained faithful, she found favor with Boaz. She was blessed with protection and food, and, eventually, Boaz became her husband. Her life was not easy. She had suffered greatly and had given up much. But she still chose to remain faithful to Naomi and the Lord through it all.

delight

How do you observe God's faithfulness in this story?

Read through Ruth 2 again. List out all the ways Ruth was blessed by the Lord.

display

God chooses to bless people through the actions of others. Ruth was blessed by Boaz and offered food and protection. Jot down one way you have been blessed by others. Then, name one way you can be a blessing to someone else.

Think about the girls in your student ministry or small group. Talk with them and come up with one way you all can work together to be a blessing to someone else soon. (It's a great idea to get your parents, guardians, or leaders involved too!)

> **Think about people who have been a blessing in your life. Then, thank God for their faithfulness to Him. Ask Him to show you how you can be the same type of blessing for others.**

Faithful

day 24

FAITHFUL CHARACTER

discover

READ RUTH 3:1-13.

Then he said, "May the Lord bless you, my daughter. You have shown more kindness now than before, because you have not pursued younger men, whether rich or poor. Now don't be afraid, my daughter. I will do for you whatever you say, since all the people in my town know that you are a woman of noble character." —Ruth 3:10-11

It's often been said that true character is revealed when we think no one is watching. Who we really are at our core, not necessarily who others perceive us as, is our character. How we make decisions, our moral integrity, and the convictions we exhibit all reveal the type of character we possess. And God always knows our true character.

Ruth was known as a woman of character by Boaz and the people of their town. They observed her work ethic, her faithfulness to Naomi, and her desire to serve the Lord. Though her life was plagued by tragedy, her character was proven strong and was fueled by her faith. As she obediently listened to Naomi, she also faithfully trusted God would provide a family redeemer.

Our faithfulness to God is also revealed in our character. When we remain morally upright under pressure or treat others with kindness, we are proving we have more than surface level character. Character that is built on trusting God and remaining faithful to Him provides us with an everlasting hope (Rom. 5:3-4). Just as Ruth found hope in a family redeemer, our character builds hope in the ultimate Redeemer, Jesus.

delight |

What are some ways your character reflects the character of Christ?

How has God used trials to build your character as you remain faithful to Him?

display |

The story of Ruth shows us that God was at work in her story, faithfully moving to help her build the type of character that could stand against trials. Think about how God's own faithfulness has been at work in the building of your character. Name one character trait that God has developed in you through the various trials you have experienced.

Take a minute to examine your heart and life. Journal about some ways you struggle to reflect the character of Christ. Are you tempted by gossip, anger, or unkindness? Do you exclude others or focus only on yourself? Take a few minutes to pour your heart out on the page. Then, focus your heart on God in prayer.

> **Ask God to help you continue to build the character of Christ in your own life. If you are walking through a trial, ask God to redeem it like He did with Ruth's struggles.**

Faithful

day 25

GOD ALWAYS HAS A PLAN

discover

READ RUTH 4:13-17.

The neighbor women said, "A son has been born to Naomi," and they named him Obed. He was the father of Jesse, the father of David. —Ruth 4:17

Taking a look at the bigger picture of Ruth's life, we see the hand of God piecing together all her struggles for good. Ruth was able to remain faithful because God was faithful. His faithfulness was at work to unveil His plan not only for Ruth, but for future generations.

Here is this Moabite woman God chose to become the mother to Obed, who would one day become the grandfather to King David. Not once did God abandon His plan or forsake Ruth and Naomi. God's faithfulness to Ruth brought her a husband and a son, and He used the events of her life to bring forth the Savior of the world. She was not a forgotten widow. She was a daughter of the most high God and a woman of faith whose offspring would be the King of Kings. God's faithfulness is always revealed in His perfect plan.

Even when we're in a place where we can't grasp how God's faithfulness is working to reveal His plans, we must trust Him and remain faithful. We cling to His Word and believe that He is working in thousands of ways we may not be able to see. His plans may not always be what we expect, but they are always for our good. We can have every confidence that the same faithfulness God showed to Ruth will also be shown to us, because we are His through Jesus.

Lifeway Girls | Devotions

delight

Why is it tough to surrender to His plans and believe that even if things do not turn out how we might expect, God is still faithful?

What is God's ultimate plan for your life? How can we trust His plan will unfold? (See 1 Thess. 5:23-24)

display

Ruth's life probably didn't turn out how she expected. When she married her first husband, she might have imagined a long life with him and lots of children. But God had different—better—plans.

How are you trusting God with the plans for your life? Write one way you can rest in God's faithfulness even when things do not turn out how you might expect.

Reflect on unexpected blessings that have come from unexpected or difficult places in your life. Name one way God has already shown you His faithfulness through a situation that didn't quite turn out how you expected.

Ask God to help you trust in His plan, even when it's different from yours.

day 26

AS OURSELVES

discover

READ 1 SAMUEL 18:1-4.

Jonathan made a covenant with David because he loved him as much as himself.
—*1 Samuel 18:3*

In this final section, we'll direct our attention to the importance of being faithful in friendships. One of the strongest examples of friendship in the Bible is that of Jonathan and David. Here we have the son of King Saul, who was an enemy of David's, forming a covenant of friendship with David because he loved him as much as himself. This covenant promise from Jonathan meant that he would be there for David through thick and thin. He would not bail or toss their friendship aside when things got tough. Rather, his love for David would be revealed through his faithfulness to their friendship, even in the most dangerous of times.

What we see in the friendship of Jonathan and David is a fulfillment of the second greatest commandment. Jesus told us that we are to love our neighbors as ourselves (Matt. 22:39). A faithful friend fulfills this commandment and demonstrates the gospel through her relationships.

Friendships can be hard at times. But we can love one another even when there might be strains on a friendship. We can choose to forgive, overlook an offense, and be gracious. We can choose to be faithful friends who desire what is best for the girls God places in our lives. Our faithfulness to love others reflects Jesus to the world and creates a sweet aroma of gospel grace.

delight

Who are the girls God has placed in your life? How are you being faithful to these friends?

Why is sacrifice important in a friendship? How does it show true love?

display

Jesus said "No one has greater love than this: to lay down his life for his friends" (John 15:13). Jesus' sacrifice shows the greatest measure of love a friendship could offer, and He calls us to do the same. He commands us to love one another. Think about how you might show your love toward the girls you're closest to this week. List two ways can you honor them above yourself.

> **One way you can love your friends is by praying for them. Take a moment to pray for your friends and your friendships. Ask God to help you be a friend who loves at all times.**

Faithful

day 27

SPEAK WELL OF EACH OTHER

discover

READ 1 SAMUEL 19:1-7.

Jonathan spoke well of David to his father, Saul. He said to him, "The king should not sin against his servant David. He hasn't sinned against you; in fact, his actions have been a great advantage to you." —1 Samuel 19:4

The tongue can be a force for good or a weapon of evil. As Jesus reminded us, the words we use reveal what is in our hearts (Matt. 15:18). Gossip, unkind words, and even crass jokes not only expose the sinfulness of the heart, but can also harm friendships. A faithful friend is a girl who seeks to speak well of others and uses words to build others up.

Jonathan spoke highly of David in hopes of persuading Saul to not kill him. He first spoke of David's righteousness. David had not sinned against Saul. Saul had no reason for David to die. Jonathan also spoke about how David's actions had been good for the king. All David had done honored Saul and was for the good his kingdom. When David slayed Goliath, it was an action that showed he was willing to risk his life for the king and his country. Through the power of his words, Jonathan was able to persuade Saul to see David in a new light. Friends always speak well of each other.

David and Jonathan's friendship is a wonderful example to us, but it is not the ultimate example. Jesus is our perfect friend who never sinned or spoke a lie (1 Pet. 2:22). Jesus always used His words to point His friends toward truth and encourage their faith. May we seek to be a friend like Jesus.

delight |

When has one of your friendships been harmed by hurtful words? Explain.

How does Jonathan's friendship with David teach you to be a good friend to the girls in your life?

display |

How can you encourage your friends this week through the power of your words? Write out three ways you can strive to be a faithful friend who speaks well of others.

For every unkind or negative thought you have about someone today, try to replace it with a truth from Scripture or by sharing kind words instead.

> **Read Psalm 141:3, pray over it, and memorize it. Make this your prayer when you are tempted to speak poorly of someone.**

day 28

FRIENDS PROTECT

discover

READ 1 SAMUEL 20:30-42.

When the servant had gone, David got up from the south side of the stone Ezel, fell facedown to the ground, and paid homage three times. Then he and Jonathan kissed each other and wept with each other, though David wept more.
—1 Samuel 20:41

David and Jonathan's faithful friendship was forged through the fires of persecution. Saul relentlessly pursued David's life, even to the point where he tried to kill his own son. Jonathan was so grieved and angry regarding his father's evil actions toward his best friend that could not even eat. But Jonathan never abandoned David—he set out to protect David at all costs. Jonathan knew God would honor his effort to protect David, even if that meant he would suffer the wrath of his father. Jonathan remained faithful to David because he knew his father's actions were evil and that David was a righteous man.

We should seek to protect our friends as well. Our faithfulness toward them is revealed when we seek to offer help or protection in their time of need. While we often think of protection in terms of avoiding physical harm, acts of protection may also include emotional or spiritual safety. If our friend is in danger of going down a road that might lead her toward emotional harm, we should speak love and truth into her life. If we observe that our friend is walking toward sin, we should point her back to the gospel. We may find that protecting a friend will cost us. Yet, true faithfulness sacrifices in the best interest of our friends.

Lifeway Girls | Devotions

delight |

What stands out to you about Jonathan's faithfulness to David in these verses? How is Jonathan a picture of Jesus' faithfulness toward us?

Give an example of how protecting a friend might cost you.

display |

When we think about protecting our friends, that doesn't mean crossing the line into sin for them. In fact, our desire should be to help them avoid sin. One of the hardest things to do is to confront our friends when they've veered into the wrong lane. If you have a friend that has strayed from the Lord, commit to pray for her and ask God to give you an opportunity to have a conversation with her where you can gently and lovingly encourage her back toward God and His grace.

> **Spend some time in prayer thanking God for your friends and asking Him to be their ultimate protector. Then, ask Him to help you be a faithful friend who is willing to protect others.**

Faithful

day 29

ENCOURAGE(D)

discover

READ 1 SAMUEL 23:15-18.

Then Saul's son Jonathan came to David in Horesh and encouraged him in his faith in God, saying, "Don't be afraid, for my father Saul will never lay a hand on you. You yourself will be king over Israel, and I'll be your second-in-command. Even my father Saul knows it is true."
—1 Samuel 23:16-17

David spent years trying to escape Saul's pursuit. During this time, Jonathan remained a faithful friend and desired to help David flee from his father. In these passages, we find that faithful friends seek to encourage each others' faith in God.

After years of running from Saul, we can imagine how weary David was growing. The Psalms testify to David's fear and exhaustion as he sought the Lord to save his life time and time again. At just the right time, Jonathan encouraged him to keep trusting God. He told David not to fear, but to hope in God's faithfulness. He reminded David to remember God's promise to anoint him as the rightful king (1 Sam. 16:13). These words were a much needed balm to David's weary soul.

We need to surround ourselves with friends who point us to trust in the Lord and hold fast to His Word. We need to be friends who encourage others in their faith. The Bible reminds us that our faith is tested so that we won't grow weary (Heb. 12:3; Jas. 1:3). During such times, we need to be friends and have friends who, as Paul said, mutually encourage each others' faith (Rom. 1:12).

Lifeway Girls | Devotions

delight |

When have you needed encouragement from a friend? How did she encourage your faith?

Why is reminding the girls we know to look to the person and work of Jesus the best encouragement we can give?

display |

Sometimes the best way to encourage the girls around you is to let them know that you understand how they feel. If you have a friend who is going through something that you have been through, seek her out and encourage her by telling her your story. Encourage her by letting her know how your faith helped you get through your difficult time.

> **Name two girls you're close with. Pray over these friends, asking God to help you be a faithful encourager to them this week.**

day 30

HAND IN HAND

discover

READ 2 SAMUEL 9:1-7.

David asked, "Is there anyone remaining from the family of Saul I can show kindness to for Jonathan's sake?" —2 Samuel 9:1

God's promise was fulfilled and David became king over Israel. Even after Jonathan died, David wanted to honor their friendship and keep the covenant they made to each other (1 Sam. 20:15). This faithful commitment to honor his friend led David to show kindness to Jonathan's crippled son, Mephibosheth. The love he had for Jonathan was shown through kindness to his family. In spite of all Saul had done to David, Mephibosheth was welcome to eat at the king's table all of his days, and Saul's land was restored to him.

Even though Mephibosheth was Jonathan's son, he was still part of Saul's family. However, David did not hold a grudge. He did not retaliate with vengeance. Rather, he honored his friendship with Jonathan and showed kindness. True, faithful friends will always seek to respond with kindness and desire to honor one another.

Kindness is not only a mark of a faithful friend, but is also a fruit of the Spirit. When God comes to live in and through us, He transforms our hearts to seek to be kind to one another. Even when we disagree, we can speak with kindness and choose to love each other. Even when a friend has wronged us, we can respond with forgiveness. Choosing to be kind is to model the character of Jesus. After all, it is the kindness of the Lord which led us to Him and toward repentance (Rom. 2:4).

delight |

What are some ways you have shown kindness to a friend or a friend has shown you kindness?

What makes it hard to show kindness at times? How can you fight against the temptation to be unkind?

display |

Scripture tells us to "be kind and compassionate to one another, forgiving one another, just as God also forgave you in Christ" (Eph. 4:32). God has showed kindness to us through Jesus. We were enemies with God before faith in Christ, yet even then God showed kindness to us. How much more should we show kindness to those who are our friends? As we show kindness to our friends, we display the same kindness God has shown to us and reveal to the world a relationship transformed by the gospel. Name two of your closest girl friends and list one way you can show kindness to each girl this week.

> **Pray for God to fill you with the kindness of His Spirit, understanding that faithfulness and kindness go hand in hand.**

Lord, set up a guard for my mouth; keep watch at the door of my lips.

PSALM 141:3

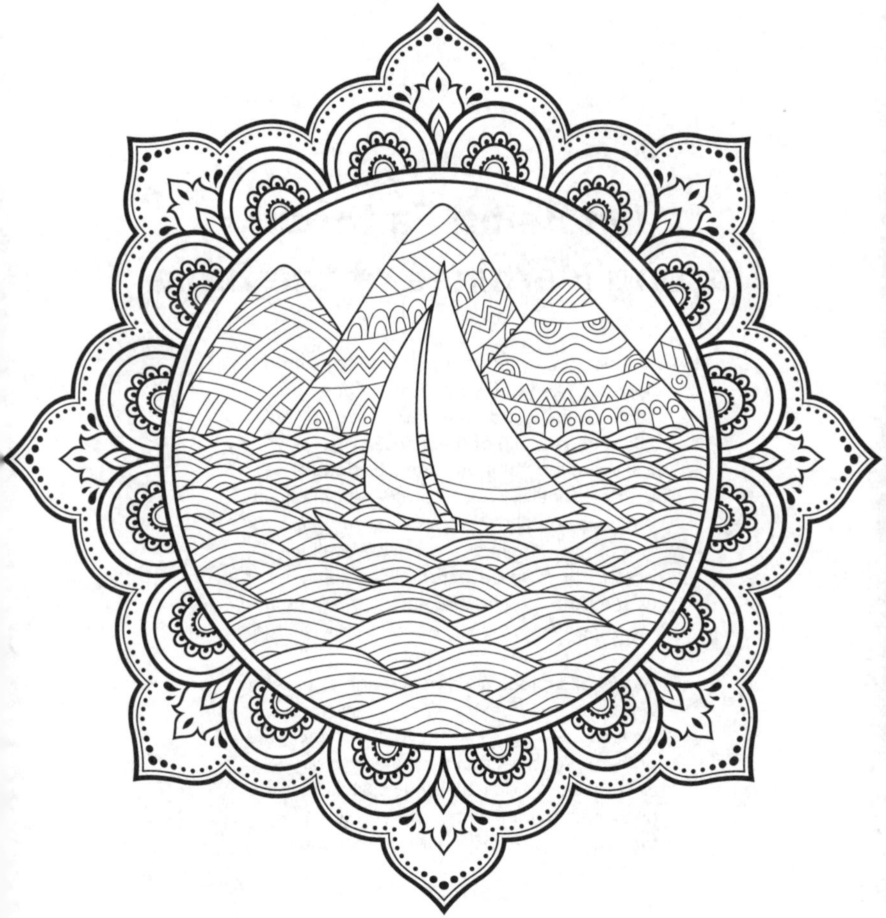

On Being Faithful: Unsung Heroines of the Bible

Maybe you've heard of personality inventories (or tests) like the Myers-Briggs, Enneagram, DISC, or the Clifton Strengthsfinder. If you've taken one (or all!) of these tests, you know they ask you a bunch of questions to determine your personality type or profile. A personality profile is not all encompassing, but helps you and others understand your personality a bit better. They can be incredibly useful in helping us see both the areas where we're strong and the areas where we still need to grow a little.

As we take a look at some women of the Bible who exemplified extraordinary faithfulness, we'll create a personality profile for each one of them. Read each of the given passages about these biblical heroines and answer the questions that follow to help you get a feel for who they are and what role they played in God's story.

Leah

Read Genesis 29:16-17, 23-25, 30-35 and 30:9-21.

Who was she?

What words would you use to describe her?

How do you see her faithfulness to God displayed?

Where does she fit into God's story?

Rahab

Read Joshua 2:1-8; 6:17-25; and Matthew 1:5.

Who was she?

What words would you use to describe her?

How do you see her faithfulness to God displayed?

Where does she fit into God's story?

Hannah

Read 1 Samuel 1.

Who was she?

What words would you use to describe her?

How do you see her faithfulness to God displayed?

Where does she fit into God's story?

Deborah

Read Judges 4:1-14; 5:1-15.

Who was she?

What words would you use to describe her?

How do you see her faithfulness to God displayed?

Where does she fit into God's story?

Mary
(the Mother of Jesus)

Read Luke 1:26-56.

Who was she?

What words would you use to describe her?

How do you see her faithfulness to God displayed?

Where does she fit into God's story?

Anna

Read Luke 2:36-38.

Who was she?

What words would you use to describe her?

How do you see her faithfulness to God displayed?

Where does she fit into God's story?

While some of these women may not be from Bible stories you're familiar with, they each played a key role in God's story. This is encouraging for every single person on earth—no matter what your home life might be like, your social status, or how popular you think you want to be, you have a unique gift and purpose that can be used for God's glory and furthering His kingdom.

How can you embrace the role God has given you today?

Stone by Stone: Remembering God's Faithfulness in Every Moment

When we're in the middle of life—the joys and stresses, the lazy days and the busyness—it can be tough to recognize God's faithfulness. But it's always there. How do we move from missing God's faithfulness to recognizing it? Let's take a look at what the Israelites did under Joshua's leadership.

Read Joshua 4.

While the priests were in the middle of the Jordan, God instructed Joshua that one man from each of the 12 tribes should take a stone from the Jordan and set them up in their camp as "a sign among [them]" (Josh. 4:6). Then, Joshua returned to where the priests were standing to set up 12 stones in the middle of the Jordan as well (Josh. 4:9). These stones were set up there to be a sign; to be a reminder to the Israelites and their children of the Lord's faithfulness and strength; that He held back the water so they could cross the river on dry ground (Josh. 4:21-24).

They set the stones up to help them remember God's faithfulness.

Set aside or move away from anything that might distract you. Close your eyes, take a deep breath, and really focus on how God has been faithful to you in all the moments leading up to this. Using the "stones" on these pages, sketch images of or journal about specific times God has been faithful to you. If you love being outdoors, consider going outside and setting up your own stones of remembrance. Whatever you do, spend some time thanking God for His faithfulness as you draw, write, or place each stone.

Lifeway Girls | Devotions

Faithful

Together in Faithfulness

Although God gave us plenty of examples throughout the Bible of His faithfulness and that of His followers, He also uses the girls around us today to show us His kind of faithfulness. When we look at the lives of faithful people, we might list their characteristics as strong, truthful, unshakable, steady—they have real staying power. These girls don't go away when the going gets tough. Instead, they're more likely to stand beside you in whatever comes, be it laughter and joy or tears and sorrow. They are there on your best days and on the days when you maybe haven't been as kind—and they'll tell it like it is.

Take a few minutes and think about your life. Do you have friends, family members, mentors, or leaders like this? Name any girls that come to mind, then thank God for each one of them specifically.

Look over your list of names of faithful girls in your life. Consider the times these girls have shown you faithfulness. Then, list any common themes that emerge. (I.e. were most of the girls on your list kind and patient?)

Lifeway Girls | Devotions

Now, ask the Holy Spirit to guide you as you examine your heart: Are you that type of faithful friend or daughter?

The truth is that we're all growing in Christ-likeness—and faithfulness—every day. We all have Jesus' righteousness working through us, but we aren't perfect, so we'll always have room to grow.

Think about all the biblical truths and stories of faithfulness you've read over the last 30 days. Think about the wonderful, faithful girls God has placed in your life. Take a few minutes to list or journal about three specific ways you would like to grow in faithfulness based on what you've learned from other godly, faithful people.

Faithful

Endnotes

1. "How Far Away Is the Moon?," NASA (NASA, September 30, 2019), https://spaceplace.nasa.gov/moon-distance/en/.
2. Charles Haddon Spurgeon, *The Metropolitan Tabernacle Pulpit*, vol. 34 (United Kingdom: Passmore, 1888), 222.
3. "Map of The Journeys of Abraham (Bible History Online)," Ark of the Covenant - Bible History Online, accessed February 22, 2021, https://www.bible-history.com/maps/6-abrahams-journeys.html.